SOUTHSIDE SLANG

Southside Slang

*A Dictionary of Southside Virginia
for Yankees, City-Slickers,
and Other Oatsiiiders*

Written by Southside Natives
Cindy Schmidt and Josh Waltman

Artwork and Layout
Julie Elms

ISBN: 9781790394296

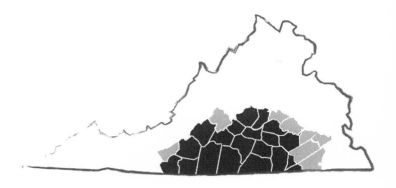

Southside Counties

Amelia, Appomattox, Bedford, Brunswick, Buckingham, Campbell, Charlotte, Cumberland, Dinwiddie, Franklin, Greenville, Halifax, Henry, Lunenburg, Mecklenburg, Nottoway, Patrick, Pittsylvania, Prince Edward, and Sussex

Other counties that have historically been linked to Southside include Amherst, Chesterfield, Floyd, Powhatan, Prince George, Southampton, and Surry.

Gittin' Start'd

What is Southside?

Southside is the region of Virginia located in the lower center portion of the state that is typically known for its rural farming culture. Tobacco has traditionally been the predominant crop; however, that industry has declined in the area in recent years. The Southside area is in the heart of the Piedmont region of Virginia. It is not coastal nor is it mountainous. It mostly consists of gently rolling hills with pastoral scenes.

People in Southside pride themselves on hospitality, faith, family, work ethic, and simple living. One of the area's claim to fame is creating Brunswick stew, which traditionally included meats such as squirrel but is now generally made with chicken. Some varieties in Southside may include beef or sheep. The region is also deeply steeped in history with Colonial historic homes; the site of the famous Patrick Henry and John Randolph of Roanoke states' rights debate; antebellum plantations; Civil War battlefields, including the surrender ground in Appomattox; significant Civil Rights sites; and more.

Identifying the counties which comprise the Southside area can be challenging since there is no clear agreement among primary sources. For this book, we have chosen to focus on the core counties that comprise the tobacco-growing area as identified by those which are part of the Tobacco Region Scholarship established in 2002 by the Virginia Tobacco Region Revitalization Commission. These counties include Amelia, Appomattox, Bedford, Brunswick, Buckingham, Campbell, Charlotte, Cumberland, Dinwiddie, Franklin, Greenville, Halifax, Henry, Lunenburg, Mecklenburg, Nottoway, Patrick, Pittsylvania, Prince Edward, and Sussex. Other counties that have historically been linked to Southside include Amherst, Chesterfield, Floyd, Powhatan, Prince George, Southampton, and Surry.

Why We Wrote this Book

We are among the few in our place of employment who are natives to the Southside region. We found that when talking to each other, we would slip into our "native tongue," so to speak, and employ colloquialisms and pronunciations that were common to us. When our colleagues would overhear us, they were often equal parts amused and baffled by some of our "talk." After a number of these encounters, we began to joke that we should write a dictionary to translate for the Yankees, city-slickers, and other oatsiiiders with whom we worked.

As we mulled over the idea of writing a book, we began to think more seriously about documenting the language and culture of the region. Traditionally, the area has been very insulated with few native Southsiders moving far away and few new people moving into the community. Often Southsiders would marry other Southsiders and would settle down very close to home. In fact, it was traditionally frowned upon by family members for Southsiders to move much farther than a neighboring county. Additionally, many Southsiders never traveled far from home, with some never even leaving the county in which they were born.

As society has become more transient and as more people were attracted to rural, low-cost living in Southside, the population has become more diverse. While that diversity adds much in the way of enriching the community with new cultures and customs, it has also begun to dilute the traditional aspects of what it has meant to be from Southside. As such, we decided to make an effort to preserve some of the pronunciations, words, phrases, foods, and other unique aspects of the culture for future generations. This book is our attempt at accomplishing that goal.

Clarifying Points

A few clarifying points may be helpful as you enjoy diving into the language of Southside. First, terms in this book are not necessarily unique to Southside. Many are used in other Southern communities, and all are not necessarily used throughout the Southside region. However, it is likely that if you spend much time in the area, you will hear many of these terms.

It also may be helpful for you to know if you are classed as a Yankee, city-slicker, or oatsiiider. If you're not sure, you probably fall into one or more of those categories. A Yankee is someone who was born and/or raised north of the Mason-Dixon Line or in a state that fought with the Union during the Civil War, sometimes referred to as the War of Northern Aggression in Southside. A city-slicker is anyone who is more accustomed to urban than rural living, and an oatsiiider is anyone who is not native to the Southside region for at least a few generations.

It is important to note that while we took a humorous approach to the book, we are in no way poking fun at or belittling the community. In fact, we are both very proud to be native Southsiders. We enjoy the colorful expressions and creative pronunciations of our hometowns. As academic librarians, we want to embrace the culture while also dispelling misconceptions that people from Southside, and the South in general, are "backwards," uneducated, or uncultured.

As you explore the rest of the book, it may be helpful to note that each dictionary entry will include four parts:

1. **Word** or phrase spelled phonetically
2. **Definition** with part(s) of speech and definition(s) in standard English
3. **Yankee translation** with an interpretation in Yankee terminology
4. **Example** with the word or phrase used in a Southside slang sentence

Definitions

Ain't no sense in that

Definition
A phrase used to express strong disapproval of someone's actions

Yankee translation
This term is used to describe an action or decision, especially in excess, that isn't warranted based on the situation at hand.

Example
Betty Jo went off on Bo infronta ev'rybody, and there just ain't no sense in that.

Ain't no way

Definition
An expression used to signify disbelief

Yankee translation
This expression does not denote implausibility or impossibility, but it signifies disbelief in the occurrence of a particular situation or action.

Example
I heard that Buddy was trying to court Mary Anne, and there jus' ain't no way she'll agree to be seen riding 'round with him in that jacked up truck.

As busy as a bull in a new heifer lot

Definition
adj. a state of extreme busyness

Yankee translation
Typically there is one bull placed in a lot with heifers, and as such, he is very busy providing "companionship" for all of them.

Example
We were swamped at work today. I was as busy as a bull in a new heifer lot.

Bacca (back-uh) or
Tabacca (tuh-back-uh)

Definition
n. Southside term to describe plantin',
growin', choppin', pullin', hangin', curin',
sellin', dipin', chewin', and smokin'
products made from tobacco

Yankee translation
This term is used to reference not just the
tobacco plant but also all stages of growth
and maturity as well as the products made
from the plant. Please note that when ripe,
tobacco is pulled and not picked in Southside. If you ask a farmer if he's picking tobacco, you will have clearly identified yourself
as an oatsiiider.

Example
*My bacca's 'bout ready to pull, but with all this
rain we've been gettin' lately, it's too muddy to git
in the fields.*

Bacca-ology

A heritage of raising tobacco is one common denominator throughout Southside. This is now a waning industry, and the region is finding a need to diversify crops and explore new agricultural revenues. Despite this transition to new crops, there are still a number of tobacco farms and terms related to the industry which are commonly used throughout the area. In fact, many Southsiders take pride in having developed their strong work ethic in a tobacco field.

Terms related to raising tobacco:

1. **Bacca worm/horn worm**–invasive green, plump worm with a horn that eats tobacco leaves, necessitating pest management by farmers
2. **Balin'**–Some flue tobacco buyers require that the cured leaves be baled when brought to market. (Dark tobacco is typically tied rather than baled.)
3. **Buck barn**–bulk tobacco barns; typically long, rectangular structures in which flue tobacco leaves are hung in order to be fire-cured, generally with propane
4. **Choppin'**–the act of using a hoe to chop out grass or weeds between plants
5. **Curin'**–drying out leaves so that they turn from green to yellow/gold

(Continued on next page)

6. **Ground leaves**–bottom three to four leaves on a tobacco plant that are typically the hardest to harvest because the field workers have to bend all the way to the ground
7. **Layin' it by**–2/3 of dirt in the row is put up against the plant the last time that it is plowed
8. **Packin' shed**–place to sort through the tobacco and bale/box it after curing it
9. **Pullin'**–the act of harvesting leaves from the plant, typically three or four at a time starting from the bottom up
10. **Rackin'**–transferring of leaves from the trailers on which they have been harvested to a metal rack in the barn
11. **Slide row**–the row in the field that does not have any plants because it is designated for the tractor and trailer
12. **Spearin'**–using a spear stick to gather dark tobacco by chopping the stalks and then spearing them onto the stick for hanging and curing
13. **Sprayin'**–treating the plants to keep the sucker from growing back once the plant has been topped and/or to treat for insects
14. **Stick barn**–traditional, old-style barns where one would string the tobacco on a stick and then hang it in the rafters for curing
15. **Tabacca barn**–special enclosed trailers on concrete used for curing dark and burley tobacco (The dark tobacco is fire cured while the burley tobacco is air cured.)

Terms related to using tobacco:

1. **Chew/plug/wad**–the lump of tobacco that one places in his mouth
2. **Chewin'/dippin'/takin' a dip**–the act of placing tobacco in one's mouth in order to absorb the nicotine and flavor
3. **Chewin' tobacco/dip/snuff**–a form of smokeless tobacco that is typically placed inside the lower front lip
4. **Spit cup**–a vessel in which one spits out the extra salvia produced from the tobacco; typically an empty soda bottle, red Solo cup, or other readily disposable container

Bibs

Definition
n. a popular article of clothing worn by farmers and other men in Southside, usually made of denim and with attached shoulder straps that connect to the base of the garment with buckles (can be worn with or without a shirt)

Yankee translation
This is not something you place around a baby's neck when she is eating.

Example
I'm gonna put on a fresh paira bibs before I head to town.

Everyone Gets Blessed in Southside . . . Well, Sorta!

The context, tone, and intention of the speaker all give clues to the meaning of this expression. It can be a genuine expression of concern and sincerity, but it can also be an insult. The insinuation is that both people in need and people that are idiots could use blessing. If the information following or preceding the expression is gossipy in nature, it is likely an insult. A soft inflection in reference to a serious matter such as a health issue indicates a genuine concern. This phrase is often used in conjunction with shaking one's head back and forth. The more vigorous the shaking of the head, the greater the degree to which the person needs to be blessed, whether sincerely or sarcastically. The more modifiers in the expression, the more likely it is to be an insult.

- Bless 'em
- Bless his/her heart
- Bless his/her little heart
- Bless his/her pea-picking little heart

Blue blazes

Definition
n. a term used to express extreme disapproval

Yankee translation
This term is used as a more polite word to denote the location of eternal damnation. As you may know, the hottest part of the flame is the blue part since that is the area of the flame with the most oxygen.

Example
What in the blue blazes were you thinkin' runnin' round half neck-ed in that getup?

Bound to

Definition
adv. a term used to identify something as inevitable

Yankee translation
This has nothing to do with actually binding something.

Example
If you keep huntin' those coons outta season, you're bound to get caught sooner or later.

Britches

Definition
n. a term for clothing that is worn below the torso and has two legs

Yankee translation
This is not the formal type of riding breeches. It's just a synonym for pants.

Example
He ain't nuthin' special. He puts on his britches one leg at a time just like the rest of us.

Buggy

Definition

n. a term used for a shopping cart

Yankee translation

While you may see Amish buggies in several areas of Southside, the term is generally not used to designate a vehicle pulled by horses. Locals will typically say "Amish buggies" when referencing horse-drawn transportation.

Example

We got a messa people coming over fer the pig-pickin' so we're gonna need to get a buggy to git all the groceries.

Catawampus

Definition
adj. askew; not as it should be

Yankee translation
This doesn't have anything to do with striking a feline.

Example
Ever since I went muddin' my truck's alignment has been all catawampus.

Cotton pickin'

Definition
adj. socially acceptable substitution for an expletive denoting a negative sentiment

Yankee translation
This is not a racial term as some may assume. It references that picking cotton is an unpleasant and back-breaking task.

Example
You've lost your cotton-pickin' mind if you think I'm gonna buy one of them little foreign cars.

Couldn't hit the broad side of a barn

Definition
A phrase signifying inaccuracy, usually in reference to aim

Yankee translation
Shooting or striking the side of a farm building is not actually being discussed when this term is used.

Example
The scope on that rifle is so catawampus that I couldn't hit the broad side of a barn if I was standin' two feet away from it.

Courtin'

Definition
v. a term used to refer to serious dating that is likely to lead to marriage, usually among young people

Yankee translation
This has nothing to do with a judge, gavel, or jury.

Example
He's been courtin' her pretty hot and heavy for a while now.

Crank up the car

Definition
v. to turn on the ignition of an automobile

Yankee translation
Some may think this involves turning up the volume on the car's stereo, but it simply means to start the car. This is likely a throwback to the days of turning an actual crank on the front of the car in order to start the engine.

Example
There's alotta frost on the windshield so you better crank up the car a few minutes early.

You Just Don't Understand!

Some Yankees and oatsiiiders think that because we talk slow, we are uneducated hicks. We (usually) know proper grammar, but you just don't understand our rules, which are surprisingly complex. Many of us are even bilingual and can speak non-Southside to converse fluently with oatsiiiders. Keep in mind that you may think we talk funny, but 'round here, you're the one who sounds funny to us. Remember the old sayin', when in Rome (or Southside), do as the Romans (or Southsiders) do.

One basic rule is to never pronounce the "g" on words ending with gerunds. This means you would say goin', meetin', talkin', and walkin', but you do pronounce the "g" if it is not a gerund such as thing, ring, and bring. Another key pronunciation rule is to always add extra vowel sounds to the middle of words. A phonetic expression of nine is niiiine, and dog is dawg. There are also other localisms such as Andy Griffin instead of Andy Griffith and Star Track instead of Star Trek.

Here is a samplin' of a few words that you may not understand when you hear them if you aren't used to pronouncing things the Southside way:

- **Aught**–ought
- **Aunt**–aunt (Okay–give us credit. We *actually* get this one right. Your mother's sister is not an ant.)

(Continued on next page)

- **Battry**–battery
- **Camra**–camera
- **Couda**–could have
- **Dawg**–dog
- **Diddy**–daddy (This varies by location in Southside but is often heard.)
- **Evah**–ever
- **Git**–get
- **Gowan**–go on
- **Hafta**–have to
- **Heepa**–heap of
- **Heerd**–heard (Rhymes with beard; Not to be confused with herd as in a herd of cattle)
- **Hid**–head
- **Idinit**–isn't it
- **Jest**–just
- **Moontens**–mountains (This one varies by area within Southside, but it is most frequently heard in the western part of the Southside region.)
- **Momma**–mom
- **Ne'er**–never
- **Nawl**–no
- **Oal**–oil
- **Oat**–out
- **Offa**–off of
- **Orta**–ought to
- **Own**–on

(Continued on next page)

- **Patayta**–potato
- **Pea-can**–pecan (This one varies and is sometimes pronounced pea-kahn when used as an adjective. For example, "I need to pick up some pea-cans cuz I'm supposed to make a pea-kahn pie for Thanksgivin'.")
- **Pilla**–pillow
- **Rasslin**–wrestling
- **Riiighcheer**–right here
- **Shooda**–should have
- **Sich**–such
- **Sed**–said
- **Shore**–sure
- **Swolt**–swelled
- **Taint**–ain't (is not)
- **Waughnt**–want
- **Wheel barrel**–wheel barrow
- **Whitchu**–with you
- **Wooda**–would have
- **Wridden**–written

Critter

Definition
n. a term used to reference an animal or a person who is not well-groomed or refined

Yankee translation
This does not reference pets but rather wild animals. In reference to a person, it usually signifies a disheveled person who is uncouth.

Example
Critters keep gittin' into my trash barrel before I git a chance to haul it off to the dump.

I can't believe she's datin' that critter. She could do so much better.

Crumb snatchers/Curtain climbers/Cry sacks

Definition
n. young children

Yankee translation
These are among a number of humorous derogatory terms for young children that are used in jest and not with actual negative intent.

Example
Your wife is pregnant again? How many curtain climbers are y'all gonna have? You already got a half dozen 'round here. You goin' for a whole litter?

Just What the Doctor Ordered

This is a sampling of medically-inspired terms that are frequently used in Southside.

- **Crop dust**–the result of flatulence released in close proximity to someone else
- **Nature's calling**–a need to relieve oneself
- **Quick step**–the manner in which one travels to the restroom when they "got the runs"
- **Root rot**–sexually-transmitted disease
- **Runs (got the runs)**–diarrhea
- **Stump your toe**–stub your toe

Current

Definition
n. electricity

Yankee translation
While the term current may be used to reference current events or water currents, in this context it is being used to discuss electrical current coming into one's home.

Example
You got your current back on? It took three day for me to get mine after that storm!

Cut the light off (or on)

Definition
v. a directive to turn off (or on) a light switch

Yankee translation
This has nothing to do with severing electric lines.

Example
Cut off the lights and close the door when you leave so the bought air don't get oat. You know money don't grow on trees 'round here.

Directly

Definition
adv. a term indicating a relatively soon manner (according to one's own priorities)

Yankee translation
This has nothing to do with directions.

Example
I'll get to that directly; it's not the biggest fish I need to fry right now.

Don't get your knickers in a twist/ panties in a wad

Definition
An expression conveying a need to relax and not take the situation at hand so seriously

Yankee translation
This has nothing to do with bunched up underwear.

Example
Don't get your knickers in a twist; I'll get to it directly.

Don't make me no difference/Don't make me no mind

Definition
An expression indicating indifference, whether due to apathy for the situation or lack of relevance

Yankee translation
We understand this expression contains a double-negative, but it is considered a politer way to say, "I don't care."

Example
My wife told me that she was gonna leave me if I went fishin' today, but it don't make me no difference because she'd drown in a heavy rain anyways. (See "She'd drown in a heavy rain" on page 79.)

Down the road a piece

Definition
A colloquialism that indicates distance relevant to the context of the sentence

Yankee translation
This has nothing to do with a piece of land or a section of the road. Locals intuitivly understand the exact distance when this expression is used even though that distance will vary based on context.

Example
If you're looking for Jimmy, you need to go down the road a piece and turn at the white church.

Draws

Definition
n. regular underwear, excluding lingerie

Yankee translation
This has nothing to do with art or creativity.

Example
What's with these yunguns these days with their pants hangin' down and their draws showin'?

Eat like a horse

Definition
v. to be gluttonous; to consume an unhealthy, large volume of food

Yankee translation
This does not pertain to eating grass or grain, or the manner in which one is chewing. (In case you city-slickers are not aware, horses will literally eat nonstop if food is constantly available to them. In fact, there is an old wives' tale that they will actually eat themselves to death.)

Example
She's swolt up like a tick because we took her to Golden Corral, and she ate like a horse.

Far piece

Definition
adj. a term signifying a measure of distance, relative to the context and locale in which it is used

Yankee translation
This has nothing to do with a piece of something. It is simply a way to indicate distance that is farther than "down the road a piece."

Example
You got to go a far piece to git to the nearest Winn-Dixie if you want an orange Chek soda and some nabs. (See "Nabs" on page 54.)

Fella

Definition
n. a positive term for a male; a good guy;
a boyfriend

Yankee translation
This term has morphed from fellow to feller
to fella.

Example
*My daughter brought her new fella over, and I
made sure I was cleaning my 12-gauge when he
got there.*

Fetch something

Definition
v. to retrieve an item

Yankee translation
This has nothing to do with playing a game
with your dog.

Example
*Can you go fetch me a cold one outta the fridge?
And don't forget to cut the light off in the kitchen.*

Southside-World Problems

You've heard of Third World problems and First World problems. Now we're going to tell you about Southside problems that people from other areas may not encounter. As with people from throughout the South, oatsiiiders may assume that we are dumb because we talk with our own dialect, often including contractions which are unique to our area. Additionally, common expressions used in Southside may not employ proper grammar, which is not an indication of our lack of awareness of proper grammar but more of a cultural norm. In fact, if you are a local who always speaks with proper grammar in Southside, you may be considered as acting uppity. Before you get judgmental about our grammar, we expect you to assimilate when in our community just as we assimilate and speak properly when in other venues.

People often have difficulty understanding us because we tend to add several extra vowels to the middle of words such as niiiine instead of nine. We also tend to blend words together such as "gowan" for "go on" or "youwaughnto" for "you want to." Southsiders usually cut off the ending of words, especially the ending "g" for gerunds such as goin', fixin', and doin'. This obviously makes using voice-to-text technologies very difficult for Southsiders . . . at least until someone invents Southern Siri.

Fetching

Definition
adj. to look attractive

Yankee translation
This also has nothing to do with playing a game with your dog.

Example
She sure does look fetchin' with that new hairdo.

Few cards short of a full deck

Definition
adj. a colloquialism for a lack of intelligence

Yankee translation
This has nothing to do with poker or any other type of card game.

Example
Bless his heart. He's a good fella, but he's a few cards short of a full deck.

Fine as frog hair

Definition
adj. high-quality; miniscule distinction

Yankee translation
This has nothing to do with an amphibian's
hair folicles. (For those city-slickers who may
not know, frogs do not have hair.)

Example
*That apple pie is as fine as frog hair; it goes down
smooth and warm.* (*See* "Apple Pie" on page 69.)

Fixin' to

Definition
v. making preparations to execute an action;
a statement of intent to begin an activity

Yankee translation
This has nothing to do with repairing
something.

Example
*I'm fixin' to tan yer hide if you don't git over
yonder and finish pullin' that bacca.*
(*See* "Tan yer hide" on page 87.)

Folks (fokes)

Definition
n. relatives (when used with a personal pronoun); people (when used without a pronoun); specific group of people (when used with an impersonal pronoun)

Yankee translation
Just a heads up, context means everything with this word.

Example
The girl brought her fella home to meet her folks. He went home and told his mama that those folks are crazy! And she said most folks are crazy nowadays.

Giggin'

Definition
v. frog hunting

Yankee translation
The term does not necessarily reference a performance by a band nor does it reference an obscene hand gesture. The act of stabbing the frog is called gigging it.

Example
That boy is so redneck that he took his girl giggin' on their first date.

Country Boy or Redneck?

The terms country boy (or girl) and redneck are often used interchangeably by oatsiiiders, but they are not the same at all to many people in Southside. Oatsiiiders should be aware of the negative connotation of redneck before using the term. Traditionally, these terms were synonymous and referred to someone whose neck gets sunburned from working outside. However, over the years the definition has become more nuanced.

A *country boy* is someone who takes pride in his rural, Southern heritage. He is well-versed in outdoor activities such as hard work, fishin', huntin', trucks, and other blue-collar pastimes. He is also the kind of person who values being neighborly, mannerable, and family-oriented. To use a phrase often quoted in Southside, "He'd give you the shirt offa his back."

While a *redneck* may have many similar interests and skill sets, he is typically more uncouth and less polished. Rednecks will often be known by their sleeveless t-shirts, junked up yards, and tacky taste. They tend to have a propensity to drink heavily, be loud, and proudly display "the flag" without regard to how it might be viewed by oatsiiiders and others who do not view it as symbol of heritage.

While a *redneck* will not be offended to be called a *country boy*, many *country boys* will be highly offended to be called a *redneck*.

Gits my goat

Definition
v. the act of successfully annoying someone in an extreme manner

Yankee translation
This has nothing to do with inheriting a farm animal in a relative's will.

Example
He was tryin' to git my goat, but it don't make me no difference.

Go all the way around the barn

Definition
A manner of explaining something that should be simple in a convoluted manner

Yankee translation
This does not actually involve walking around a farm building.

Example
Talkin' to her just tires me out e'ry since she got a fancy college education! She can't ever say anything directly; she has to go all the way around the barn to git to her point!

Good grief

Definition
An expression of exasperation

Yankee translation
This does not indicate mourning in a healthy manner.

Example
Good grief! She throws a hissy fit over the least little thing.

Great day

Definition
An expression that encapsulates either the dual concepts of surprise and frustration or surprise and excitement, depending on the context in which it is used

Yankee translation
This does not reference a postive 24-hour period of time.

Example
Great day! I can't believe we won those free tickets to the tractor pull.

Great day! I can't believe the prices on those John Deeres; I guess we'll have to stick with our Farmall.

Grinn' like a possum

Definition
A facial expression indicating mischievousness or extreme joy

Yankee translation
The term plays homage to both the personality as well as the distinctive facial characteristics of an opossum which makes them appear to be smiling.

Example
When she said yes to his proposal, he was grinin' like a possum all day, and his brother was grinnin' like a possum, too, cuz he's already plannin' on trashin' their truck on the weddin' day.

Gussied up

Definition
adj. fancy attire

Yankee translation
This is likely a derivative of gussets, which is also a clothing-related term.

Example
She was all gussied up in her Sunday go to meetin'
clothes when she was headin' to preachin'.
(*See* "Sunday go to meetin" on page 74.)

Hankerin'

Definition
n. a desire or craving, typically referring to food

Yankee translation
This has nothing to do with a man named Henry or handkerchiefs, which we pronounce hane-ker-chifs.

Example
I have a hankerin' for some Brunswick stew.
I heard that that stew master Charles is fixin' it
at the fire department this Saturday.

Hard row to hoe

Definition
Expression referring to a difficult aspect of a task or period of life

Yankee translation
This is in reference to rows in a tobacco field that are particularly grassy and difficult to maintain by the farm laborers.

Example
Missy's got a hard row to hoe. Her husband has been steppin' out on her, her mama's been sick, and her yungun is as wild as a buck.

He fell outta the ugly tree and hit ev'ry branch on the way down.

Definition
Phrase used jovially to describe someone who is extremely unattractive

Yankee translation
Just so you know, we don't actually have ugly trees in the South. All of our trees are attractive.

Example
I can't believe she's datin' him. I mean he fell outta the ugly tree and hit ev'ry branch on the way down. Bless his heart.

Non-food Foods

You can't necessary take words at face value when in Southside. For instance, many words that sound like they are about food may not actually be. In fact, some of these are downright unappetizing. As stated in other areas, it's all about context.

- **Cow patties**–the solid, mounded excrement of a cow
- **Good gravy**–an expression of surprise or exasperation
- **Honey**–term of endearment used with loved ones (i.e., grandmas or spouses) or by someone in a service industry with their customers (i.e., waitresses, hotel clerks, etc.)
- **Mud pies**–a playtime activity for children that involves filling an old pie plate with mud and letting it dry in the sun
- **Now you're cookin' with Crisco**–a state of accomplishing a task effectively
- **Plum**–an adjective that intensifies the noun that it modifies (i.e., plum crazy or plum fabulous)
- **Sugar or Shuug**–*see* Honey
- **Sweetie pie**–*see* Honey

Heard tell

Definition
v. to repeat news that has been shared with you without divulging the source of that information

Yankee translation
This does not necessarily imply that the person was gossiping, but it may. As Southerners will often say, you tell names or tales but not both at the same time. Of course, there is also the other Southern expression, "If you don't have anything nice to say, come sit by me." So, once again, the interpretation of this is subject to the context and the person using it.

Example
I heard tell that Harley was datin' a Yankee girl and that his folks were pitchin' a fit!

Heavens to Betsy

Definition
An expression of exasperation

Yankee translation
This does not necessarily mean that someone named Betsy is going to make it through the Pearly Gates.

Example
Heavens to Betsy, that child is a brat; he threw a hissy fit in the middle of preachin'.

Hen pecked

Definition
adj. a state of a man being controlled, badgered, or bullied by his wife or girlfriend

Yankee translation
This references the fact that hens will peck other chickens in order to show dominance.

Example
He's so hen pecked that it's no wonder he's goin' bald.

High cotton

Definition
n. affluence; wealth

Yankee translation
This does not refer to linen thread counts. This beckons to the time when farmers' wealth was measured by the success of their crops. The higher the cotton, the greater the yield.

Example
Sammy acts like he's in high cotton now that he's drivin' 'round in his fancy new truck, but everybody knows he's still livin' in the trailer with his momndem. (See "Yer momndem" on page III.)

High on the hog

Definition
[1] extravagant or affluent lifestyle; [2] situational use of an aspect of an extravagant or affluent lifestyle

Yankee translation
This does not necessarily have anything to do with strapping a saddle on a big pig to ride him. It is a term referencing that the meats that are higher up on a pig are the ones that are typically viewed as more desirable and expensive.

Example
Ev'ry since the Smiths won that lottery jackpot, they have sure been livin' high on the hog.

You must think you're livin' high on the hog tonight since you're eatin' steak.

Hissy fit

Definition
n. an exhibition of poor behavior as the result of an ill temper

Yankee translation
This has nothing to do with the athletic ability of a snake.

Example
Ain't no need to throw a hissy fit. I'll get to it directly.

Things Y'all Might Eat 'Round Here

There are some foods that are common to Southside but that may be unfamiliar to oatsiiiders.

- **Brunswick stew**–tomato-based meat and vegetable stew typically cooked in large outdoor "stew pots" by a local "stew master" with a recipe that has been handed down for generations. The stew is often sold as a fundraiser for local fire departments, churches, and huntin' clubs.
- **Chittlins**–pork intestines which have been cut into small sections, fried, and often eaten with hot sauce (This term is also sometimes used to refer to children.)
- **Cracklins**–homemade fried pork skin that is similar to pork rinds
- **Deer meat**–venison (If you say venison, people will know that you are an oatsiiider, or if you're a local, they will think you're gittin' above yer raisin'.)
- **Drink**–soda; soft drink; co-cola
- **Dumplin'**–bread dough that has been cooked in a liquid (i.e., chicken 'n dumplins; apple dumplins) This term is also sometimes used as a term of endearment for a child.
- **Fatback**–the fatty meat from the back of the pig which is often added to beans for flavor or baked with the rind on

(Continued on next page)

- **Fried apple pies**–individualized, special variety of apple turnovers with homemade dough and fruit filling
- **Hoe cakes**–bread dough fried that everyone's grandma makes
- **Hogjaw**–hog jowl; cheeks of a pig that are cut in strips and fried (or baked) and eaten like bacon
- **Limas**–a type of butter beans commonly grown in Southside
- **Mater**–tomato
- **Moon pies**–a store-bought marshmallow and chocolate dessert
- **Nabs**–store-bought crackers with a filling such as peanut butter or cheese that come in packs of six
- **Scratchers**–chicken feet (or lottery tickets)
- **Snaps**–green beans; string beans (Freshly picked green beans make a snapping sound when you break them into smaller sections for canning or cooking.)
- **Tater**–potato
- **Tater cakes**–leftover mashed potatoes that have been pattied out and fried
- **Veye-een-a-s**–vienna sausages

Hoot

Definition
[1]*adj.* when used in combination with a form of the verb "to be": fun, energetic, or rambunctious; [2]*adv.* when used in combination with a form of the verb "to give": apathy; [3]adj. used to describe an owl

Yankee translation
In this context, the term is not used as a form of onomatopoeia in reference to the sound an owl makes.

Example
I don't give a hoot if that hoot owl keeps you up all night cuz you're always such a hoot when you're tired.

Housecoat

Definition
n. a modest article of clothing worn by women over their nightgowns

Yankee translation
This does not reference jackets worn indoors because someone is too cheap to heat the house properly. Men wear robes, but women may wear robes or housecoats. Robes are generally considered to be of higher quality or something that would be acceptable to be worn in front of house guests.

Example
She answered the door in her housecoat and slippers with rollers in her hair.

Hush up/Highsch up

Definition
A stern directive to be quiet that can be used ironically with friends or when scolding someone

Yankee translation
This does not involve being quiet on the upper floors of a library.

Example
When dad told me to highsch up, I knew I'd better listen before I got my hide tanned.
(*See* "Tan yer hide" on page 87.)

In a bind/In a pickle

Definition
A difficult or precarious situation

Yankee translation
This has nothing to do with imprisonment.

Example
It's been raining for a week, my tractor's broke, and I lost all my help. Now I'm in a bind to get the crops in.

Itchin'

Definition
n. excited to do something that you have wanted to do for a long time

Yankee translation
This does not necessarily mean that you have a mosquito bite or rash that is irritating you.

Example
Ev'r since I bought my truck, I've been itchin' to put a lift kit on it.

Culinary-Inspired Expressions

Food is an important part of culture in Southside, and as such, many expressions are derived from the supper table.

- **Slow as molasses** (on a cold Sunday morning) – very slow (Molasses is thick and pours slowly anytime but especially on a cold morning. Sunday mornings are typically a slower pace than other mornings.)
- **If you can't take the heat, stay out of the kitchen.**–Avoid situations that you can't handle.
- **Pig pickin'**–a gathering that is centered around slowly roastin' a whole pig in a large outdoor smoker
- **Dinner**–lunch (Depending on who you're talking to, dinner can be the evening or lunch-time meal. Often, older people refer to lunch as dinner; others call it supper if eating at home and dinner if dining out.)
- **Eats or eatin'**–food (You may hear expressions such as "Thems good eats" or "That's good eatin'" when referring to home-cooked meals.)
- **Supper**–*see* dinner
- **Sobbing/sopping**–to soak up remaining gravy or juices on your plate with your bread and then eat it

Jackleg

Definition
[1] v. to repair something in a manner that is subpar and only utilizing the minimum amount of effort necessary to complete the task; [2] n. a person who jacklegs something

Yankee translation
This has nothing to do with someone named Jack who has a prosthetic lower limb.

Example
The John Brown electrical wiring in our house is always on the fritz because the electrician jacklegged the whole job.

John Brown

Definition
adj. derogatory term referencing something that is annoying

Yankee translation
This is not referencing a contemporary person, but it does play homage to the notorious John Brown raids in the antebellum South culminating at Harper's Ferry, Virginia.

Example
See previous entry

Kewinkie dink

Definition
n. coincidence

Yankee translation
This does not refer to a cream-filled, oblong-shaped yellow snack cake.

Example
What a kewinkie dink running into you at the grocery store pickin' up supplies for the Brunswick stew at the fire department this weekend!

Kick the pig

Definition
v. to depart at the conclusion of a day's work

Yankee translation
This has nothing to do with abusing a farm animal.

Example
Once I finish gittin' up these last hay bales, I'm gonna kick the pig . . . good and hard.

Healthy Cookin' the Southside Way

In Southside, we can take even the healthiest foods and make them unhealthy. We love to batter and fry things, especially vegetables such as squash, zucchini, okra, tomatoes, and green beans. Some things get fried with or without battering such as apples, taters, squash, zucchini, onions, and peppers. We also like to fry things that are already unhealthy like Oreos, Twinkies, and apple pies. Of course, don't forget fried chicken. No family gathering or church covered dish meal is complete without fried chicken. Basically, the culinary technique of choice, regardless of the food item, is to smother it in butter and/or fry it.

Knee high to a grasshopper

Definition
An expression signifying small stature

Yankee translation
This has nothing to do with measuring the height of a grasshopper's knees.

Example
Lawd have mercy! The last time I saw you, you were knee high to a grasshopper, and look at you all grown up now!

Lible

Definition
adj. inevitable

Yankee translation
This is a different pronunciation for liable, but in Southside Virginia, you would never pronounce the "a" unless you want to be considered uppity.

Example
His lies were lible to catch up with him sooner or later.

Lick

Definition
n. a negligible amount

Yankee translation
This has nothing to do with applying one's tongue to something.

Example
He ain't done a lick of work in a month of Sundays. My momndem told me not to marry him cuz he won't worth a lick.

Light out

Definition
v. to depart

Yankee translation
This has nothing to do with extinguishing a candle or turning off the electricity.

Example
"Grandma, I gotta light outta Sunday lunch early cuz I got a date."

Lightnin' bugs

Definition
n. fireflies

Yankee translation
This does not refer to Zeus's favorite insect.

Example
I got a whole jar full of lightnin' bugs! Wanna see?

Little red wagon

Definition
n. a problem of one's own making

Yankee translation
This has nothing to do with Radio Flyers.

Example
That's their little red wagon; they're gonna hafta to pull it all by themselves.

Madder than a wet hen

Definition
adj. extreme anger

Yankee translation
This refers to the practicing of dunking broody hens in a water trough.

Example
Man, my momma was madder than a wet hen when I came home last night three sheets to the wind. (See "Three sheets to the wind" *on page 69.)*

Make hay while the sun is shinin'

Definition
v. to capitalize on an opportunity while one is able to do so

Yankee translation
This references the fact that farmers cut and bale hay when it is dry and daylight. Wet hay will mildew and be useless for feeding farm animals.

Example
I heard she just broke up with her boyfriend so I'd better make hay while the sun is shinin'.

Intoxicating Language

With few social activities in rural communities, drinking, including home brewed beverages, is a common pastime. As such, there are a number of alcohol-related terms that may be frequently heard in the communities of Southside.

- **Apple Pie**–a variety of moonshine that has an apple flavor
- **Drunk as a skunk**–to be very inebriated
- **If you can't run with the big dogs, stay on the porch.**–Don't attempt to drink the same amount as people who can out drink you.
- **Jacked up**–drunk
- **Lit up**–drunk
- **Mountain Dew**–moonshine
- **Toddy**–an evening alcoholic mixed drink that is typically consumed by genteel elderly church ladies after the evening meal (A hot toddy is slightly different and references a home remedy for a sore throat that includes whiskey, honey, and lemon juice.)
- **Three sheets to the wind**–*see* Drunk as a skunk
- **White lightnin'**–moonshine

Mosey

Definition
adj. to travel in a leisurely or lazy manner, depending on the context in which the term is used

Yankee translation
This has nothing to do with the manner in which Moses' basket traveled down the Nile in the Bible.

Example
I've got the whole day off so I think I'll mosey on down to the flea market and see if they've got anything good today.

Muddin'/Rootin'

Definition
v. to gallivant in a four-wheel-drive truck or all-terrain vehicle in a muddy landscape

Yankee translation
This has nothing to do with digging up the roots of a plant.

Example
Me and my buddies are going muddin' on the farm tonight to get ready for the Mud Bog this weekend.

Necked (neck-ed)

Definition
adj. the state of being unclothed while being amorous or doing something mischievous

Yankee translation
This pronunciation has a different connotation than naked which is purely describing someone who is nude, regardless of their activity. For instance, if one is alone in the shower, they are naked; if they have company with them, they are necked.

Example
She was naked taking her shower the morning of her wedding, but she was necked taking her shower that evening.

Gettin' Religion

Religion is an important part of the culture in Southside. As such, it only makes sense that it would be incorporated into the vernacular of other aspects of life.

- **Come hell or high water**–no matter what happens
- **Could make a preacher cuss**–a situation, circumstance, or person who has generated extreme frustration
- **Glory be**–an expression used to indicate jubilation, surprise, or exasperation, depending on the context in which it is used
- **Go over like a fart in church on Sunday**– an expression indicating that whatever is being referenced is either extremely inappropriate or will not be well-received
- **If the Lord's willing and the creek don't rise**– a statement of intent to do something barring any unforeseen obstacles
- **Lawd have mercy**–Lord have mercy; an informal request for the Lord to intervene in a situation, often used in jest
- **Month of Sundays**–long time
- **Preaching/big church**–worship service, typically the 11 o'clock service in a Southern Baptist church

(Continued on next page)

- **Sunday best**-one's most respectful and nicest clothing (Wearing your best clothes to church is considered a sign of respect.)
- **Sunday go to meetin'**-*see* Preaching/big church
- **Sweatin' like a whore in church on Sunday**-a state of extreme discomfort or nervousness
- **Y'all must not be payin' the preacher enough**-a phrase often used jokingly in discussions of drought conditions with the implication that the preacher hasn't been praying enough to influence the Lord to send rain

Neckin'

Definition
v. to engage in amorous kissing for a prolonged session, usually in a discrete location such as a parked vehicle

Yankee translation
This has nothing to do with neckties, scarves, ascots, necklaces, bowties, bolos, or other such accessories.

Example
You should only be necked when you're neckin' if you're hitched to yer fella.

Neither here nor there

Definition
Not pertinent to the current conversation

Yankee translation
This has nothing to do with being confused about the location of something.

Example
Whether it's a good deal or not is neither here nor there cuz you're not buyin' another truck to park in his yard!

Ninnie

Definition
[1]n. teat on a barnyard animal; *[2]n.* a person that lacks a keen mind

Yankee translation
This has nothing to do with a person hired to care for children nor is this Minnie Mouse's younger sister.

Example
When you milk Ole' Betsy be sure to be gentle cuz she kicks if you grab her ninnies too hard.

Ole

Definition
[1] *adj.* term expressing affection in regards to the noun it modifies; [2] *adj.* a term used to identify something that is a standard or staple item in your life or community; [3] *adj.* old

Yankee translation
This has nothing to do with a matador's shout of exhilaration when he dodges a bull.

Example
Ole grandpa had to go up and visit ole Dr. Smith, and he stopped by the ole country store on his way.

Piddlin'

Definition
adj. to proceed in one's tasks in a lackadaisical manner

Yankee translation
This does not refer to a pig that plays the fiddle nor should it be confused with the similar term piddley, which means a small amount.

Example
I'm off work today so I've just been piddlin' around in my shop.

Polite(ish) Ways to Remind Someone of Their Roots

Southsiders, and Southerners in general, pride themselves on being polite. This means that even when we are insulting or critiquing someone, we often use euphemisms to do so. The phrases listed below are examples of expressions used to call people pretentious, haughty, or pompous. These sayings are often used when a Southsider is around oatsiiiders or city-slickers and begins to pick up their language or culture rather than embracing his own culture. When this happens, it can often be interpreted as someone who is trying to appear more refined than the general population of the area. Southsiders pride themselves on simple, virtuous living without the trappings of popular culture or a desire to garner the approval of "refined" culture.

- **Above yer raisin'**–above your raising (rearing)
- **Gittin' too big for yer britches**–getting too big for your britches (pants)
- **High and mighty**
- **Highfalutin** or **high flu-tin**
- **Puttin' on airs**–putting on airs
- **She'd drown in a heavy rain**–She has her nose stuck up so high in the air that the rain would drown her.
- **Up on your high horse**–above everybody
- **Uppidee**–uppity

Pinch

Definition
[1]*n.* a small quantity; [2]*n.* an exact measurement in a family recipe; [3]*n.* a term used in a prepositional phrase describing being in a difficult situation

Yankee translation
This has nothing to do with not wearing green on St. Patrick's Day.

Example
I was in a pinch because the recipe called for a pinch of sugar, but I was completely out of that. But then momma told me I could substitute a pinch of honey instead.

Pitch a fit

Definition
[1]*v.* expressing extreme displeasure over a situation; [2]*v.* displaying a childish temper-tantrum

Yankee translation
This isn't like pitching a tent.

Example
Ms. Honeycutt said that my kid pitched a fit in class yesterday, but I'm goin' up there and pitch a fit in her office about how she picks on him all the time.

Pocketbook

Definition
[1]*n.* a lady's handbag or purse; [2]*n.* an old man's wallet

Yankee translation
This has nothing to do with works of literature that are small enough to fit in one's pocket.

Example
Let me just grab my pocketbook before we head to the beauty parlor.

50 Shades of Y'all

Y'all is a contraction for you all. Some might wonder why we say "all y'all" if y'all is already plural. That's a great question with an equally great answer. Y'all often means two or more people to whom one is directly speaking. Y'all can also reference a specific group of people in the room to whom the information is relevant, and this is indicated by the context in which it is said as well as by eye contact. Additionally, y'all can be directed to only one person in the room who is a

(Continued on next page)

representative of a larger group to whom the information is being directed. All y'all means everyone in earshot.

We know this is very confusing to you Yankees, but learning these subtle nuances is the key to fitting into our ranks. Here are some examples to help you out:

> *We want to welcome all y'all* (everyone in attendance) *to the covered dish meal here at the church this afternoon. I know some of y'all* (select group) *have been askin' aboat how the preacher has been doin' after his surgery. He wanted to let y'all* (those who have been wondering) *know that he's making steady progress and appreciates all y'all's* (everyone who has been praying for him) *prayers. I also wanted to let everybody know that the church will be over at y'all's house tomorrow* (makes eye contact with the specific church member) *to repair the fence damaged in the recent storm. Lastly, before we pray, I wanted to remind y'all* (those with young children to whom this may be of interest) *that the nursery is open for those with yunguns who need a nap.*

Poor thing

Definition
n. a person or animal that is in a difficult or
sad situation

Yankee translation
This does not necessarily have anything
to do with one's limited economic means.
The term can be used sympathetically or
sarcastically, depending on context.

Example
*I swannee, the poor thing lost her job and her
boyfriend in the same week.*

*My wife had to go to a conference in Disney
World for work. Poor thing!*

Put on your big girl panties

Definition
The act of exhibiting mature behaviors in response to a difficult or unpleasant situation

Yankee translation
This has nothing to do with needing a reminder to wear undergarments.

Example
Suck it up buttercup, put on your big girl panties, and stop complainin' about cleanin' the commode. You use it just like ev'rybody else in the house.

Rabbid dawgs

Definition
n. canines that are specifically trained to hunt rabbits

Yankee translation
This is not a reference to canines with rabies.

Example
Come on and help me load the dawg box on the truck. We got to go pick up those rabbid dawgs.

Reckon

Definition
v. to ponder or postulate about an action

Yankee translation
This has nothing to do with a reckoning such as an apocalypse.

Example
I reckon we better give a little extra to the Lottie Moon offering since we missed the Annie Armstrong one at Easter time.

Punishin' People

Southsiders have colorful expressions for many things, and with their often fiery tempers, oatsiiiders should not be surprised that many of them involve references to ways in which "physical persuasion" is used to achieve a desired end result.

- **Beat you nine ways til Sunday**-to use a variety of methods to show someone the error of their ways; typically used in jest to imply frustration
- **Box yer ears**-to strike someone's ears on both sides with cupped hands

- **Come along hold**–to pull a man in a particular direction by persuasively grabbing and holding a part of his anatomy that can be very sensitive
- **Jerk a knot in someone**–to apply force to ensure compliance (This is generally a threat rather than an actual action.)
- **Knuckle sandwich**–a fist in someone's mouth
- **Switches**–small tree limbs that are strong yet pliable; used to inflict physical force, generally to one's legs or buttocks (Many mothers in Southside use switches or fly swatters to correct the error of their children's ways.)
- **Take you out to the woodshed**–the location of getting a switchin' or whoopin'
- **Tan yer hide**–to change the color of one's backside to a reddish shade as a result of a whoopin'
- **Whoopin'**–a spanking, usually with a belt and more severe than a switchin'; beat up someone

Reyet nice

Definition
adj. surprisingly pleasing

Yankee translation
This denotes a degree of pleasure that is better than average but not extraordinarily so. It is typically used in situations where one was not expecting a pleasant experience or outcome.

Example
Well, that was a reyet nice get together even tho' Uncle Joe was three sheets to the wind.
(*See* "Three sheets in the wind" on page 69.)

Rode hard and put up wet

Definition
[1] *adj.* to appear to have been worked excessively with little care; [2] *adj.* (There's another definition, but we're just not going there cuz we're Christian folks.)

Yankee translation
This is a nod to proper care of a horse. Once they have been ridden enough to work up a sweat, they should always be brushed down before being sent back to the pasture.

Example
After a day like this, I feel like I've been rode hard and put up wet.

We Say Grace &
We Say Ma'am

If you spend any significant amount of time in Southside, you will quickly notice the prevalence of the use of terms such as ma'am and sir. For you Yankees, this does not carry a negative implication like it often does in the North. It does not always imply age, although sometimes respect is warranted because of someone's age. It can refer to position, status, familiarity, and authority. Upstanding Southsiders are taught from a young age that using these terms is a matter of respect for the person to whom they are speaking.

Here are the rules of application:

1. Always use with elders unless they are non-family members who are close friends
2. Always use when interacting with strangers in public unless they are significantly younger or you want to infer that they do not deserve respect
3. Always use with people in authority unless you want to imply that they do not deserve respect
4. Sometimes use with acquaintances, as the situation warrants
5. Never use with close friends or family unless they are elders or you are joking with them

In addition to ma'am and sir, it is typically considered good manners in Southside to call an elder Mr./Mrs./Miss followed by their last name until they give permission to call them by their first name. Sometimes, ladies will give children permission to call them Miss followed by their first name rather than their last name. This is a more personal and yet still respectful form of address. Male suitors also often refer to their dates as Miss followed by their last or sometimes first name as opposed to just using their first name alone. This is typically done early in the dating relationship or when they are trying to be playful.

Rule the roost

Definition
v. the act of being in control of one's household

Yankee translation
This references the dominance of a particular rooster in the barnyard. Sometimes chickens will actually kill roosters who compete for dominance.

Example
He needs to stop being so hen-pecked and start rulin' the roost at home.

Run it in the ground (and break it off)

Definition
v. to belabor a point to the extent that it becomes annoying

Yankee translation
This has nothing to do with drilling a hole in the earth.

Example
The whole town has been gossipin' for a month about the preacher running off with the choir director. They've run it in the ground and broke it off.

Scrape the roads

Definition
v. to plow the roads after a snow storm

Yankee translation
This has nothing to do with removing roadkill.

Example
I wish they'd come scrape my road so I can go to town and pick up some House Autry to fry up that chicken for dinner.

Scrapin' the bottom of the barrel

Definition
v. the act of selecting from among limited, and perhaps undesirable, options

Yankee translation
This has nothing to with engraving or cleaning the barrel of the gun.

Example
The high school sure was scrapin' the bottom of the barrel to put a team together this year. Bless their hearts, they haven't won a game all year.

Skoesh

Definition
n. a miniscule amount relative to the situation at hand

Yankee translation
This is not a brand of baby clothes.

Example
Can you move the sofa over a skoesh?

Shindig

Definition
n. a party or event that is celebratory in nature

Yankee translation
This has nothing to do with hitting your shin while digging a hole.

Example
They sure didn't throw much of a shindig for the weddin' reception. I reckon they wanted to keep it simple so they could head off to the honeymoon faster.

Slim pickins

Definition
n. an undesirably small amount from which to choose; a limited selection

Yankee translation
This has nothing to do with skinny people picking the banjo.

Example
It sure was slim pickins at the grocery store cuz ev'rybody cleaned it out at the first sign of snowflakes.

Smidge

Definition
[1]*n.* a precise amount when cooking such as a pinch; [2]*n.* a small amount relative to the context in which it is used

Yankee translation
This has nothing to do with little people, sometimes derogatorily referred to as midgets, crossing a smooth bridge.

Example
Don't forget to add a smidge of bakin' soda to your sweet tea to keep it fresh.

So good make you slap yer momma down the creek and fuss at her for gettin' wet

Definition
Phrase indicating something that is so extremely good and desirable that you want to proclaim it broadly

Yankee translation
This has nothing to do with abusing your elders in a current of water. (This is something that no self-respecting Southsider would ever do. It is an excessive exaggeration to convey a level of extreme excitement.)

Example
He said that the pig pickin' was gonna be so good that it would make you want to slap yer momma down the creek and fuss at her for gettin' wet.

Stubborn as a mule/Mule-headed

Definition
adj. an extreme level of obstinance

Yankee translation
This expression is derived from the fact that mules are notorious for refusing to do as directed.

Example
Coworkers have told the authors of this book that they are as stubborn as mules.

Swanney

Definition
v. to express surprise or exasperation

Yankee translation
This has nothing to do with pigs or swine. While this can be used interchangeably with the word swear, it is not used as a cuss word.

Example
I swanney, if I find another snake in the chicken house, these chickens are all gonna be on the supper table come Sunday.

Sweetie

Definition
[1]*n.* a term of endearment used between acquaintances or sweethearts;
[2]*n.* condenscending term used to patronize someone who is upset; may be used interchangeably with sweetheart, sweetie pie, or shuug

Yankee translation
This has nothing to do with a dessert that is high in calories.

Example
Now sweetie, there's no need to get your panties in a wad over it.

Tennis shoes

Definition
n. athletic shoes

Yankee translation
This does not mean a specific type of athletic shoe used to play the game of tennis. It refers to any and all types of athletic shoes. (Before you Yankees judge us, ask yourself why you call them sneakers; most of them squeak too much to actually sneak up on someone.)

Example
Hang on a sec and let me change into my tennis shoes if we're goin' to town.

Too big for your britches

Definition
adj. a phrase used to describe a Southsider who is acting in a haughty manner that is not customary among their relatives and acquaintances

Yankee translation
This does not mean that a person has gained weight and needs to purchase a larger size of pants. The action that is being described may be perfectly acceptable in some social contexts but not when done so around other Southsiders.

Example
After he came back from college, my son was actin' too big for his britches, actin' like he's too good to git dirty workin' on the farm.

Too many chiefs, not enough Indians

Definition
Phrase indicating that there is an overabundance of those trying to lead and a lack of those willing to follow

Yankee translation
This is a similar phrase to "too many cooks in the kitchen."

Example
The problem with the church buildin' committee is too many chiefs and not enough Indians.

Two bricks shy of a full load

Definition
Phrase indicating a lack of intelligence or
poor judgment

Yankee translation
This is not a phrase used by masons—free
or otherwise.

Example
*When he went to back his boat into the water, he
backed too far and flooded his truck. He must be
two bricks shy of a full load.*

Two shakes of a lamb's tail

Definition
A phrase used to indicate a rapid response

Yankee translation
This has no direct connection to a salt shaker a milkshake, or a ewe. The expression comes from how quickly a lamb can shake its tail.

Example
I swanney! Keep yer britches on. I'll git to it in two shakes of a lamb's tail.

Ugly

Definition
adj. mean-spirited

Yankee translation
This does not reference one's level of
physical attractiveness. Instead, it relates to
one's actions, intentions, or words that are
less than desirable.

Example
*Betty told me that my son was two bricks shy of
a full load. It may be a little true, but she didn't
have to be ugly aboat it.*

Well, I declare

Definition
[1]Phrase that indicates frustration; [2]a phrase expressing surprise; [3]to acknowledge, yet gently disregard, a statement from another

Yankee translation
This has nothing to do with giving orations or creedal statements.

Example
Well, I declare. I ain't ne'er heard of sich a thing in my whole life!

Wet behind the ears

Definition
adj. inexperienced

Yankee translation
A person's personal hygiene habits are not the focus of this phrase.

Example
That boy is so wet behind the ears that he don't know a carburetor from a spark plug.

What for

Definition
n. a verbalized expression of consternation to a specific person

Yankee translation
Contrary to the popular vernacular, this is not used as a question.

Example
If he talks to my momma that way, I'm gonna give him what for.

What the world?

Definition
A socially-acceptable euphemistic phrase to express shock, irritation, or disgust

Yankee translation
This is not the beginning of a geographic question nor does it have to do with intergalactic travel.

Example
What the world? I thought you were a country boy. Why are you listenin' to that head-banger music?

Whippersnapper

Definition
n. a young person who is arrogant and overly confident

Yankee translation
This is not the latest Girl Scout cookie flavor.

Example
I'm gonna jerk a knot in that little whippersnapper if he talks back one more time.

Whoopin'/Switchin'

Definition
[1]*n.* a beating; [2]*n.* spanking; [3]*adv.* failure at a task

Yankee translation
This does not refer to eating a whoopie pie.

Example
My dad said that if I let somebody whoop up on me one more time, he's gonna give me the whoopin' of my life when I get home. But my football practice is whoopin' me so bad that I don't have the energy to put up much of a fight.

Yer momndem

Definition
n. a family clan consisting of immediate relatives that include one's mother and other relatives living in close proximity or who are relationally close

Yankee translation
In Southside, most families live around each other and have many meals and social events together with the oldest female relative being recognized as the matriarch.

Example
Are you goin' down to yer momndems for Sunday lunch? We're plannin' to git the kids together for a game of whiffle ball and croquet.

Yonder

Definition
n. a location relative to the person using the term

Yankee translation
This could be a short distance or a long distance, depending on the context in which it is used; it could be anywhere from feet to miles. (Southsiders inherently understand the amount of distance being expressed. We even have a popular hymn, "When the Roll Is Called up Yonder.")

Example
Why don't you go over yonder and start picking up those limbs for me while I run up yonder to the store and grab some gas for the lawn mower?

You know what side of yer bread's got butter on it

Definition
A phrase indicating awareness of the prudence of acting kindly and respectfully to those who take care of you

Yankee translation
Don't take this literally. No one is insulting your ability to detect condiments on your baked goods.

Example
If you know what side of yer bread's got butter on it, you'll get those gutters cleaned out before you go fishin'.

Yungun

Definition
¹*n.* a child; ²*n.* youngest person in a group

Yankee translation
This is an amalgamation of the words "young" and "one." It could be used matter-of-factly or in a condscending manner.

Example
I did substitute teaching the other day, and those yunguns just ain't got no raisin' these days.

f Connect with us.
Facebook.com/Southsideslang
or southsidevaslang@gmail.com

Tell us what you liked, what you
didn't like, and what things we
forgot to include.

About the authors

Cindy and Josh are librarians and native Southsiders. Cindy was born and raised in Lunenburg County and then moved to Prince Edward and Charlotte Counties. Josh is a native of Pittsylvania County who later relocated to Campbell County after a brief attempt at city-living in Lynchburg. Both Cindy and Josh grew up in rural areas surrounded by tobacco fields and livestock.

 Cindy currently lives in Cullen, Virginia, with her husband, two sons, two dogs, and three cats.

 Josh currently lives in Rustburg, Virginia, with his wife, two tame cats, and a large feral cat colony.

Made in the USA
Lexington, KY
06 December 2019